CASTLES OF
SCOTLAND

Colin Baxter Photography, Grantown-on-Spey, Scotland

CASTLES OF SCOTLAND

Scotland's castles are known across the world for their grandeur and beauty. Their architecture ranges from the massive, stark and austere to the light, ornate and fairy-tale in appearance. Each castle is different; some, like Hermitage, grand and forbidding, some, such as Dunrobin and Dunvegan, lively family homes, some ruinous, some enchanting, but perhaps no other feature in Scotland's landscape has left a more profound imprint of those who went before. They have been described as 'archives in stone' and so they are.

Ruinous or complete, each castle tells a story of the master builders or architects who designed them and of the masons who built them. And they tell us of the men, and sometimes women, who had these castles built as their homes and fortresses.

Most important, perhaps, is that the castles were also home and workplace to people from every walk of life. These great buildings were places of worship, courts of law, prisons, barracks, places of entertainment and hospitality. They needed bakers, gardeners, stable-hands, blacksmiths, seamstresses, cooks, musicians, armourers… The list is endless. For some, it is the almost inevitable ghost story which appeals. Whether you believe or not, would you walk the ramparts at midnight?

Depending on how they are defined there are at the very least 1200 stone castles in Scotland. Here is a selection.

◄ GLAMIS CASTLE, ANGUS

Stories of ghosts, murders, royalty and fairy-folk are common at the childhood home of the Queen Mother and birthplace of her younger daughter, Princess Margaret. The first castle was probably built some 900 years ago. Today the building is a mix of mostly 18th-century, romantic styles. Bonnie Prince Charlie and his infamous enemy, the Duke of Cumberland, stayed here separately in 1746 before the Battle of Culloden. Shakespeare, however, invented his murderous Macbeth as Thane of Glamis.

CASTLE SWEEN, ARGYLL

The oldest standing castle in Scotland. Built by the MacSweens in the late 12th century, it has been little altered. The high curtain wall rises dramatically in front of Loch Sween and the island of Jura. These stark, two-metre thick walls once enclosed a busy courtyard full of timber buildings and the bustle of everyday life.

◄ BALMORAL CASTLE, DEESIDE

Chosen by Queen Victoria and Prince Albert as a romantic retreat in their beloved Scottish Highlands. In 1853-5 the present castle was built of local white granite from the Prince's mock-baronial design. Inside, he clad several rooms from floor to ceiling in Royal Stuart and green Hunting Stuart tartan.

DUNROBIN CASTLE, ► SUTHERLAND

Family seat of the Earls, and later, the Dukes of Sutherland. Designed by Charles Barry, architect of the Houses of Parliament, the 19th-century façade was in marked contrast to the austerity of earlier strong-holds on this site since the 13th century. The ghost of the daughter of the 14th Earl, may be heard weeping.

◀ CRAIGIEVAR CASTLE, GRAMPIAN

Built by merchant William Forbes, 'Danzig Willie', it is, for some, the loveliest building in Scotland. Not completed until 1626, Craigievar follows the style of earlier tower houses. The great hall with its medieval-style vaulted roof and Renaissance decoration is an architectural jewel.

CASTLE STALKER, ARGYLL ▶

The Stewart of Appin battle cry 'Rock of the Cormorants' names the island where the castle was built for James IV around 1540. It was once lost to the Campbells in a bet for an eight-oared galley. Nearby Lismore Island is rich in archaeology and is famous for the 16th-century *Book of the Dean of Lismore*.

◀ HERMITAGE CASTLE, BORDERS

The 'Strength of Liddesdale', strategic key to the Borders, is a most forbidding castle. A fortified manor in the early 14th century, the present complex structure was largely built by 1400. The Douglas family created a tower house, added three massive towers then an even larger tower block. Despite an illness, in 1566 Mary, Queen of Scots made a 50-mile round-trip journey from Jedburgh to visit her wounded lover, the Earl of Bothwell at Hermitage. The consequent exhaustion nearly cost her her life.

DUNVEGAN CASTLE, ISLE OF SKYE

Rebuilt at least nine times, the 'Seat of MacLeod' has been inhabited by a single family for 700 years – longer than any other Scottish castle. The first chief, Leod, gained Dunvegan through marriage in the 13th century. Safe inside is the Fairy Flag. Its power to save the MacLeods from disaster three times has been invoked twice.

DUNSTAFFNAGE CASTLE, ARGYLL

Traditionally, on the fortified site of the 'capital' of the kings of Pictland and Dalriada. From here, the Stone of Destiny was taken to Scone in 843. The present ruins were the 13th-century seat of the Macdougal Lords of Lorn, though it is known for its later Campbell overlords. Jacobite heroine Flora Macdonald was briefly imprisoned here.

BLAIR CASTLE, ► PERTHSHIRE

The present 19th-century edifice hides a history said to begin in 1269 when John Comyn, Lord of Badenoch, built a tower here. Subsequently held by the Earls of Atholl, it was garrisoned in 1689 by Viscount Dundee whose body was carried to the castle after the Battle of Killiecrankie.

Blair makes claim to being the last castle to be besieged in Britain when, in 1746, Lord George Murray, brother of the Duke of Atholl, failed to win it for the Jacobites.

CASTLE FRASER, GRAMPIAN

KISIMUL CASTLE, CASTLE BAY, ISLE OF BARRA

Island home of the MacNeils of Barra, the tower house, possibly 11th century, was restored between 1938 and 1972. Tradition says that it was announced daily from the walls: 'MacNeil has dined. The Kings, Princes and others of the earth may now dine.'.

◄ STIRLING CASTLE

At the heart of Scotland, on an ancient and strategically crucial site. Mirroring the nation's history, the castle changed hands many times and witnessed innumerable royal occasions including the coronations of Mary, Queen of Scots and her son James VI, and the baptism of his first son, Prince Henry. The Royal Palace, with its finely carved Renaissance façades, Great Hall, Old King's Building and Chapel Royal form the core.

KILCHURN CASTLE ►

A picturesque tower house at the head of Loch Awe built about 1450 by the Campbells of Glenorchy, later Earls of Breadalbane. Kilchurn was substantially altered in the 1690s to accommodate the 1st Earl's private army.

◄ CAWDOR CASTLE, NEAR NAIRN

Home to the Thanes of Calder, pronounced 'Cawdor' so later spelled and popularised as such in Shakespeare's Macbeth. The massive central tower was built in 1454. It is said that the 1st Thane was instructed in a dream to let a donkey, laden with gold, wander until it lay down and there to build his castle. The trunk of the hawthorn tree where the animal came to rest is preserved in the tower.

BALLINDALLOCH CASTLE, ► BANFFSHIRE

Situated where the river Avon meets the Spey, this 16th-century Z-plan fortalice is now much extended. It has been held by the Grant family since the 18th century.

▲ Rothesay Castle, Isle of Bute   Brodick Castle, Isle of Arran ▶

◀ CAERLAVEROCK CASTLE,
DUMFRIES-SHIRE

Architecturally unique in Scotland, the ground plan of Caerlaverock is triangular. Besieged and briefly taken from the Maxwells by Edward I in 1300, it was then described as being '… like a shield, for it had but three sides round it, with a tower at each corner, but one of them was a double one…'. Although the castle was demolished soon after, the description holds true for the now ruinous, 14th-century replacement. The gatehouse has been described as the most impressive in Scotland.

INVERNESS CASTLE

Built originally in 1039, the castle was enlarged, strengthened and renamed Fort George by General Wade in 1725. It was captured and destroyed by the Jacobites in 1746, and soon after superseded by the new Fort George at Ardersier. Rebuilt in two phases, 1834 and 1846, the castle is now used as a Sheriff Court and County Constabulary Headquarters.

CORGARFF CASTLE, ABERDEENSHIRE

Austere in a stark landscape, Corgarff was burned down in about 1571 by supporters of Queen Mary. Burned again by Jacobites in 1689 and destroyed for a third time in 1746, it was rebuilt as a Hanoverian barracks two years later with a star-shaped musketry wall. Subsequently it was an outpost against the illicit whisky trade in the 19th century.

DUART CASTLE, ▶ ISLE OF MULL

The principal MacLean stronghold, Duart stands sentinel over the Sound of Mull, Loch Linnhe and the Firth of Lorn with sight-lines to the castles of Dunstaffnage, Dunollie, Ardtornish and Achadun. First built with a massive curtain-walled enclosure and timber buildings, the tower house was added in the 14th century. It came to the MacLeans by marriage in about 1367 from the Lords of the Isles. The castle was lovingly restored in the early 20th century by Sir Fitzroy MacLean.

Huntly Castle, Grampian

BALVENIE CASTLE, DUFFTOWN

A curtain-walled 13th-century castle, much remodelled by the Douglases over the next 200 years. Balvenie passed through many hands. John Stewart, 4th Earl of Atholl, transformed it into a stylish Renaissance residence. It was abandoned by the Duffs in 1724.

◀ Breachacha Castle, Isle of Coll

The tower and enclosure date from about 1435-50. From the time it was built, Breachacha was fought over by two lines of the same family – the Macleans of Coll and the Macleans of Duart – until the latter surrendered it to Archibald Campbell, Earl of Argyll, in 1679.

Urquhart Castle ▶

There has been a castle on this strategic site since the 12th century. The present, largely 17th-century, ruins tell little of the comfortable residence built by John Grant of Freuchie after 1509 with its bakehouse, brewhouse, oxhouse, dove grove, orchard and more, servicing the hall and chambers where guests slept in feather beds with bolsters, blankets and sheets.

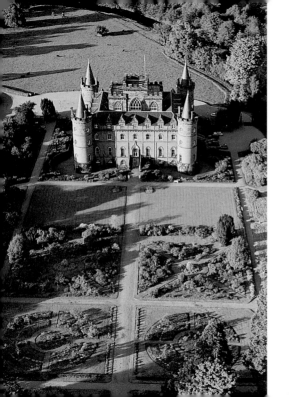

◀ INVERARAY CASTLE, ARGYLL

Several architects inspired the 18th-century mansion with its gothic features, French interiors and some of the finest neo-classical plasterwork in Britain. Victorian influence added the conical pepper pots and dormers. The site has been home to the Earls, later Dukes, of Argyll since the 15th century.

EDINBURGH CASTLE ▶

Dominating the capital, the castle is home to the Scottish crown jewels, the Stone of Destiny, site of the National War Memorial and birthplace of James VI and I, first monarch of Scotland and England. St Margaret's 11th-century chapel is the oldest part of the Castle which largely owes its appearance to a Victorian face-lift.

FYVIE CASTLE, ABERDEENSHIRE

Published in Great Britain in 1999 by Colin Baxter Photography Ltd,
Grantown-on-Spey, Moray PH26 3NA, Scotland
Reprinted 2001

Text by Lorna Ewan

Photographs & Text Copyright © Colin Baxter 1999   All rights reserved.

A CIP Catalogue record for this book is available from the British Library.

ISBN 1-84107-004-1   *Colin Baxter Gift Book Series*   Printed in Hong Kong

Page one photograph: **Crathes Castle**   Page two photograph: **Eilean Donan Castle**
Front cover photograph: **Castle Stalker**   Back cover photograph: **Eilean Donan Castle**